A MANUAL OF RECEPTIVE PRAYER:

For Study, Practice, and Retreats

A MANUAL OF

RECEPTIVE PRAYER

for Study,
Practice
and Retreats

Grace Adolphsen Brame

CHARIS ENTERPRISES
Wilmington, Delaware
2006

Publisher: Charis Enterprises, 13 North Cliffe Drive,
            Wilmington, Delaware, 19809

Cover Design and Execution: Eleanor Nichols and
                            Erin Hyland, and
                            Grace Adolphsen Brame

A MANUAL OF RECEPTIVE PRAYER: For Study, Practice, and Retreats accompanies the Third Edition (2005) of the text, now entitled: *RECEPTIVE PRAYER: Prayer Which Nourishes, Heals, and Empowers.* The text was published originally by Charis Enterprises, Wilmington, DE 19809, USA, in 1981; then by Chalice Press (CBP), St. Louis, MO; 1985. The title for those two editions was RECEPTIVE PRAYER: A Christian Approach to Meditation.

#1005 -B

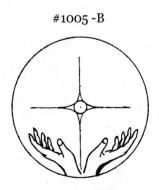

Order From:

Amazon, Barnes & Noble, Borders, or Ingram

ISBN 0-9769090-1-4

DEDICATION

You are about to begin an adventure
which will change your life;
therefore, this dedication is to
you.

Sitting in the silence,
you may ask:

"Do I want
to grow in God?"

"What will I let go of,
what will I give
to allow my heart to open?"

God wants to be ever
more real to you...
to nourish, heal, and empower you.

Would you like to be held
in God's embrace...

And to return it?

A MANUAL OF RECEPTIVE PRAYER:
for Study, Practice, and Retreats

TABLE OF CONTENTS

ACKNOWLEDGEMENTS

Gratitude must go to our wonderful Spiritual Growth Group with whom my husband, Ed, and I met for nineteen years. That growth group, in which we challenged ourselves to spiritually stretch, has deeply affected the life of every member. In those days, when not many people consciously believed in listening to God as well as speaking to God, this way of learning in the silence was sustenance for our souls, and our group was a critical personal support for its members. We eventually disbanded only because many of us had to be traveling often. Yet what we gained will never leave us. The group's use of this material and their comments, spoken from uniquely varied spiritual stances, have made a difference in how the manual is written.

A special thanks goes to Susan Blunier for thoughtful, careful typing and many helpful suggestions.

Credit For:

"Spirit of the Living God" (adaptation of the Daniel Iverson text made by Word of God, Ann Arbor, Michigan) by permission of Moody Bible Institute of Chicago. Copyright, 1935, 1963, MBI.

"Take, O Take Me As I Am" (text and music by John Bell, the Iona Community) by permission of GIA Publications, Inc. Agent. Copyright, 1995.

"Stay with Us, O Lord" (text and music by Barbara Bridges) Permission granted by Barbara Bridges. Copyright, 2002.

"I Sought the Lord" (text anonymous, ca. 1890, and music by Grace Adolphsen Brame). Copyright, 2006.

The goal of Receptive Prayer
is
to be aware of God' presence
and then
to allow God to love us,
answer us,
guide, and gently heal us.

We will *begin*
to realize what matters most and
to see others with God's eyes,
if we are open to that experience.

In the conscious presence of the One we deeply love,
we can become more and more
what we are called to be:
the vessels and channels,
the heart and hands
of God.

Yet, even though such prayer is
grace received,
we know that sometimes there will be
darkness and desert.
Then, when we cannot feel
that ever-present Life,
our trust becomes remembering
those times when it was vividly real.
It also rests on believing
what we know is true:
that we are held and enfolded
in unseen Love
which is aware of all that is beyond
our sense and sight.

INTRODUCTION

The Purposes of the Manual

... To enable individual and group study of the text,
"RECEPTIVE PRAYER: Prayer Which Nourishes,
Heals and Empowers;"
... To provide relevant scriptural sources and related hymns;
... To offer a resource useable for retreats; and
... To guide a receptive approach to life.

****

This manual is written from a conviction that *Receptive Prayer is a way to live, not just a way to worship.* The author believes that the practice of Quiet Receptive Prayer can lead to a way of living more positively and affirmatively. It can become an approach to life that recognizes that ALL of life is God's and is meant to be lived by God's power, loved for God's sake, and shared through the Spirit. This last approach is Active Receptive Prayer.

God's grace has given us the magnificent capacity to relate to God, to know and love God, and to give our lives to share what God is giving. Receptive Prayer is a way to receive the good being poured into us by the Spirit, sometimes coming to us through the prayers of others. It can enable us to feel more loved, more worthwhile and more capable of giving. As we learn to receive grace more fully, we will become less addicted to negative habits of mind, more capable of self-fulfillment, and more insightful and loving toward others.

What is about to be learned (or, perhaps learned more deeply) is not at all new in history, but it may seem new to us until we discover how we have done it unconsciously, without knowing. Then it is like discovering buried treasure that has been with us all along, but which we can now use by training ourselves, somewhat as a musician or an athlete trains: through attitude, practice, and understanding. That, it turns out, is the true meaning of *ascesis,* the word that has become "asceticism."

May the course challenge the brain and enlarge the sensitivities of each one involved. And may each be comforted and refreshed by the Spirit of Life as God becomes more and more close and real.

Who Can Use the Manual?

Anyone who will approach meditation as a form of prayer, that is, as communion with God, may find this manual helpful. It has been written especially, but not exclusively, for people with a Christian heritage, drawing deeply on the Bible and Christian hymnology.

Length of Course

A group my take seven or fourteen weeks, as desired, with one extra meeting as an introduction. An individual may choose his or her own pace as noted below.

Procedure

Whether you study by yourself, with a partner, or with a group, decide how many weeks you want to give to the course. Whether it is seven or fourteen will depend on how slowly or thoroughly you wish to proceed, or how frequently the group desires to meet.

Decide on your personal commitment. Choose a regular time and place alone, without distractions and responsibilities. Consider that what you are able to give of yourself will relate to what you will receive. Just as you take time for a wonderful meal and not only enjoy, but are nourished by it, the time for Receptive Prayer will become deeply important and satisfying to you. Praying receptively twice a day is most helpful, especially when beginning. However, if time is a problem, you may well decide to begin with far less. What matters first is to *get started,* even if it is only a few minutes!

Each of the seven weekly or bi-weekly sections has a theme such as "Breathing," "Visualizing," "Listening," or "Affirming." Each of these is divided into eight parts including:

1. Scripture readings,
2. Questions based on the scripture,
3. Readings from the text,
4. Questions based on the text,
5. Related hymns,
6. Memorization,
7. Quiet Receptive Prayer, and
8. Active Receptive Prayer suggestions.

The most important sections are the Quiet and Active Receptive Prayer. If you cannot make use of all the other material at the same time, you may divide it according to your needs. Perhaps you will read the text and questions in the morning and turn your thoughts to scripture or memorizing at night. Furthermore, there are many opportunities to be pondering just one question or memorizing a few lines while working with the hands, walking, eating, driving (if this is not distracting), or while waiting for an appointment or standing in line somewhere.

See Chapter III for thoroughly explained specifics about your own time for Quiet Receptive Prayer. Until that is read, you may do the following. If you are alone, take the phone off the hook. If others are near, explain that you wish to be undisturbed. When you are ready to enter Quiet Receptive Prayer, you may wish to set a soft kitchen timer in the next room so that you will know when your time set aside is over.

Readings of the text are purposely short so that they may be read slowly, thoughtfully, insightfully, and in prayer. Each chapter is divided into seven readings, one for each day of the week, or every two days if two weeks is allowed per chapter. *It would be helpful to mark the seven divisions of each chapter in your text.*

Underlining, writing comments, or posing questions in your text, manual, or Bible can be extremely useful. *This manual has purposely left room for your written responses to the questions posed.* Your spiritual journal may be used for even longer responses. Other supportive procedures are mentioned in the next section.

Please notice that, hereafter, "p. will indicate "page" and numbers will refer to *text* pages unless otherwise stated.

Supports

Affirmative Prayer: Note how you phrase your spoken prayers, and see when they might be more meaningful and helpful if put into an affirmative mode. Try changing the words "Please," "Help," and "Make" to "I trust," "I claim," "I receive," etc. See page 26 in the text.

Insightful Reading: *Lectio divina* (literally "divine reading") was the way of Bible reading in the early church, and has been the practice of people seeking the Holy Spirit in scripture and inspirational literature in every generation. You will find it meaningful as well. You may read visualizing that you are present when the action described took place. You may imagine that you are hearing the words, or that the words are addressed to you, if appropriate. Give yourself time to experience the passage, savoring, drinking in the words and their depths of meaning. At this point, do not analyze. Luther would have said to listen with your heart, to be one of those taught by God, i.e. one of the *theodidacti*. His comments on *lectio divina* are found on p. 38 of the text. Also see pp. 66, 67 under "Bible Reading."

Journal Keeping Some of the most inspired individuals of history have kept a spiritual journal. In it they wrote precious insights which came to them spontaneously or as they read the Scriptures, other devotional literature, or meditated. You will find this an enormously useful tool to remember your most precious understandings. *No matter how important your*

experience or insight may be, it can be forgotten in a moment, if
it is not noted!

It is a good idea to number the pages and make a table of
contents in your journal to highlight things to which you would
like to return later: Bible passages, hymns, topics, special ways
of saying something, inspirational readings, etc., with direct
bearing on Receptive Prayer and the life of the spirit. My own
favorite way is to underline or write in red one word or term
which clarifies the main point in each day's writing. Then I list
the page number and that topic in the space allowed for the table
of contents at the beginning of each journal. If you choose to do
this, when you have finished the present course, you will have
further resources to which you can turn your attention. (See p.
77) Furthermore, you will have an invaluable resource for your
speaking, teaching, or writing.

Hymns: Some of the most inspired spiritual poetry ever written is
found in hymns and psalms. When simply read quietly, they are
experienced very differently than when buoyed by music. Their
messages are not primarily intellectual but go to the heart of
spiritual experience.   They are, in fact, the result of such
experience and often are the catalyst for others to come. Whether
sung or read, they are prayers. Try both!

Actually singing hymns or psalms in private devotion is a
practice with which few are familiar. Yet leaders of all religions
have spoken of the value of the stirring of the Spirit through the
movement of music in the body. The English clergyman, William
Law, wrote a whole chapter about it in his classic: "A Serious
Call to a Devout and Holy Life," saying:

> Begin all your prayers with a psalm ... I do not mean
> that you should read over the psalm, but that you
> should chant or sing ... For there is nothing that so
> clears a way for your prayers, nothing that so disperses
> dullness of heart, nothing that so purifies the soul from

poor and little passions, nothing that so opens heaven, or carries your heart so near it, as these songs of praise ... Singing is a natural effect of joy in the heart, so it has also a natural power of rendering the heart joyful. (It is one of) the motions and actions of the body which have the ... power of raising ... thoughts and sentiments in the soul.[1]

Hymns chosen are those well enough known to be found in several collections. Page numbers for well-known hymnals are listed in Hymn Sources, pp. 100 - 106 of the Manual. The hymns may be used as desired: read or sung individually, alone, or in a group. They are chosen specifically for the theme of each section. However, some could be useful at any session, and more are suggested than can be used. You may wish to look ahead at all the resources mentioned.

Memorization: Memorization centers the mind and upholds the spirit. What is memorized one day may be the inspiration needed on another when there is no opportunity to look up an appropriate passage or when the brain and heart are too befuddled to think or act coherently. Verses of scripture flashing to mind can undergird many who teach and preach. A memorized hymn can go a long way in making a sick person well as the mind sings it over and over. A sentence which is meaningful to you may be perfect to share spontaneously with someone you care about at a moment now unforeseen. And what is memorized may well return to you as future guidance in Receptive Prayer.

Prayer Partner or Spiritual Friend: You may choose someone whom you love and trust, then pray for each other daily, perhaps at the same time. You should be able to call this person in an emergency and ask for support, even for a continued period of time, knowing that it will be given.

---

[1] Law, William. *A Serious Call to a Devout and Holy Life*, 1729. Noted in *Wholly for God*, ed. Andrew Murray, Minneapolis, MN, Bethany House Pub., 1976, pp. 249, 250.

Remembering Others: Remember at least one other person, known or unknown, each time you pray receptively, perceiving them, also, as receiving. If you are sharing this study and practice with a group, include the group as a whole or each member of the group daily in your Receptive Prayer. I particularly like to pray for some unknown person who is alone and forgotten. Another way of sharing is to sense the enfolding love of God surrounding the world, or a whole country, or a specific group of people gathered together. You do not have to be more specific than this. Such a prayer can be very powerful. Receptive Prayer feeds you and me, and it reaches out, embracing and blessing others as well.

Teacher Training: Training for teachers and group leaders will be provided by Charis Enterprises when there are sufficient requests. Please see notes at the end of the manual.

SECTION ONE

SELF-OFFERING

(Leader: See notes on "The Introductory Meeting: Manual p. 95).

Questions on beginning an adventure:

(1)   What matters most to you in this venture?

(2)   What are your hopes and goals?

(3)   What disciplines and supportive techniques will you choose to help yourself?

Scripture reading (to be read daily or as often as desired):

Luke 1: 26-38 – "According to Your Word"

Questions based on the reading:

(1)   What quality in Mary enabled her to hear or know the message of the angel?

(2)   What words of Mary indicate her attitude?

(3)   The Bible, as God's Word, or communication, often mentions God speaking to individuals and tells of the work of the Holy Spirit: guiding, teaching, and reminding; convicting, converting, and comforting; inspiring and strengthening both individuals and groups. What quality seems to have been in the people who were so affected?

(4)   What new insights, questions, feelings, or responses do you have about this passage?

Questions based on the text: (in seven groups)

Day 1: "*Foreword*" - p. 8

    a.   What does the second paragraph of the Foreword mean to me? The statement begins: "Most of us pray that God..."

    b.   Comment on the idea that pushing and pleading with God will not make our prayers come true. Why does the author say: "Only one thing may do it; that is learning to live and pray receptively?"

    c.   What does you think the statement on p. 8 means: "There is no other way to know *God's will* but to pray and live receptively?"

Day 2: "*The Gift*" - p. 13

    a.   What does God's grace have to do with the section called "The Gift?" Why does the author choose to put this here? Tournier speaks of "the greatest possible human event." Do you identify with his words or have an idea of what he means? Can you relate this assessment with the lives of various historical personages, with people whom you know, or with your own experience? What difference did it make? Was it (or has it been) a quiet, progressive experience or a climactic event at the end of a time of trial, insight, or growth?

Day 3: Short thoughts to be savored - pp. 14, 15

    a.   Since most of us pray for "answers" to our prayers, how do you respond to the suggestion of God's giving of himself as the deepest Answer?

Day 4: pp. 16-21

    a.   If Receptive Prayer is a way to receive God's answer to our needs, what do waiting, listening, yielding, changing, and allowing ourselves to be loved have to do with this process? What does self-offering have to do with receptivity? Do you see a difference between what the author calls Expressive Prayer and Receptive Prayer?

    b.   Write your *present* definition of prayer. Is it a conversation, a communication, a relationship, a communion, a realization, or do you have better words to express it?

Day 5: pp. 22, 23

    a. According to the author, can meditation be something other than Receptive Prayer? If so, what? If Receptive Prayer is a form of meditation, how does it differ from other forms? Why has the author chosen to call it Receptive Prayer?

Day 6: pp. 24-27 (Includes "Prayer has an asking side" and most of *Chapter One: "Learning to Receive the Gift"*)

    a. Do you have difficulty in receiving from others? Why is this true so often? Do you think: "I don't deserve it"? Or are you afraid someone, or you yourself, will think you weak or needy? What makes it difficult for you to receive? Training? Pride? Schedule? Too much to do, to accomplish? Fear? The guilt of "not doing anything"? The hopelessness of believing it won't work? By learning to receive, could you help yourself? Others? Could you even help God?

    b. What opportunities to receive have you, so far, not accepted? Would you consider accepting them in the future?

    c. Am I or have I ever been drained of strength, hope, or desire to love? Is (was) there anything to be received that I could (did, did not) take advantage of?

d. What is the relationship between holiness and humor?

Day 7: pp. 27, 28 "We find it easier to ask ...." to end of chapter.

   a.   Is it possible for our prayers to be answered if we do not receive? Please explain.

   b.   What other things do you particularly respond to in this section? What questions does it bring to mind? What insight or inspiration?

   c.   How are the following hymns related to the readings?

Hymns: You may *choose from* the following. Sources for these hymns and *others* are noted in the Manual on pp. 100 - 106.

"Alleluia! Alleluia!"
"Spirit of the Living God"
"Spirit of God, Descend Upon My Heart"
"Take My Life and Let It Be Consecrated"
"Take, O Take Me As I Am"

   "Take, O take me as I am; Summon out what I shall be;
   set your seal upon my heart and live in me."

"Gather Us In" (at beginning or end of any session. It has energy!)
"Stay with Us, O Lord" – (at the *end* of each evening session)

Spirit of the Living God

Spir - it of the liv - ing God, fall a-fresh on me.

Spir - it of the liv - ing God, fall a-fresh on me.

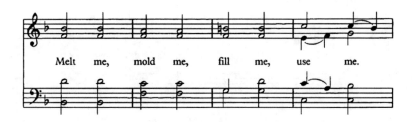

Melt me, mold me, fill me, use me.

Spir - it of the liv - ing God, fall a-fresh on me.

(For groups, a second stanza can simply replace "me" with "you." Then it becomes a song of communion in the Spirit.)

Take, O take me as I am

Take, O take me as I am;___ sum-mon out what I shall be;___

set your seal up-on my heart and live in me.___

Stay with Us, O Lord

Stay with us, O Lord, for the day will soon be

O Light of the world.

o-ver. Stay with-in us, O Light of the world.

O Light of the world.

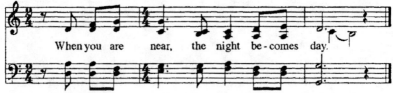

When you are near, the night be-comes day.

Memorization: The "Lord of Love" Prayer on p. 29.

Quiet Receptive Prayer: *Self Offering, the Root of Receptivity*

(Before each period of Quiet Receptive Prayer, it would be helpful to read the suggestions in this section one or two times and then proceed according to what you remember. This probably should be done every time until you feel used to it... A series of dots indicates a pause. .... If desired, in a group, the leader may use the following as a *guided* Receptive Prayer.)

Relaxing: Sitting in quietness and trust, allow your hands to rest palms up, receptively, upon your thighs... Look slightly up at a picture, a cross, the sky, or a space on the wall... Allow your head to rest comfortably, raising only your eyes... Look at the point of focus for a few moments, then into it for several more moments, then through it, and then beyond... Stay in that consciousness for a few moments. Finally, still looking slightly up, gently close your eyes... (Do this each time you meditate.)

Begin to let go of all tension, new and old... Feel a yawn at the back of your throat and think of your scalp relaxing... Allow tension to flow down and out of the body from the cheeks, then the eyes and jaw; throat, shoulders, arms, and hands; chest and abdomen; down and through legs and feet, and through the tips of the toes... Allow yourself whatever time is needed, enjoying the release, giving it to God... (With experience, this will become natural and take much less time).

Dedicating: Offer yourself and your life to God... Offer your MIND with its thoughts and focusing, its perceptions, understandings, and imaginings. Offer your EYES with their ability to see beauty and to notice people so that no one is invisible to you... Offer your TONGUE so that God's Spirit will be in the words you speak, the tone of your voice, and the intent behind your communications. Offer your THROAT and your WILL so that God's will becomes yours... Offer your SHOULDERS, your burdens and your work... Offer your HEART, your emotions and your life-giving love... Offer the PIT OF YOUR STOMACH, the center of your being. Offer in *trust*, thinking: *"I trust you, Lord, I trust."* ... Through this experience you are offering all you are to God so that you may discover and reveal your Lord through your own attitude and actions.

You will sometimes use the brief form of dedication in the "Lord of Love Prayer" which you have just begun to memorize from p. 29.

Receiving (Drinking In): Now there is no need for words... You may rest in this experience of continuous *giving of your heart and receiving life and love from God...* (This is the Still Point, the Silence, the very heart of Receptive Prayer, noted on p. 64, 69, and 74.)

Sharing: Remember at least one other whom you would bless. If you have an inspiration such as understanding them more fully, or words that would encourage or inspire, words which can be said or written, remember them.

Think of the day ahead, allowing creative ideas to come to you... Write down all you wish to remember...

Then stretch well every part of your body, enjoying the deliciousness of movement; breathe several long, deep breaths as energy builds; and finally open your eyes as though it is the first time you have ever seen. Allow yourself to wonder at the gift of sight. Notice, pay attention, see - everything around you. If there are others present, bless them with your eyes or a touch or a word... Then go on to *living your prayer* in Active Receptive Prayer.

Receptive Prayer: *Receiving from God through Others*

Throughout this first week or two, allow yourself the grace of receiving: accepting assistance, gifts, thoughtfulness, compliments, and encouragement from others as God's gifts to you, while permitting them the joy of generosity, the sharing of themselves. It is enough to say "Thank you" or "I'm grateful for your encouragement (or appreciation or support)." Try not to dismiss such acts or words of grace. Receive them as God's gifts to you through them.

SECTION TWO

BREATHING

Scripture reading:

Genesis 2: 4-7 "The Breath of God"

Questions based on the reading:

(1)   According to this account, God took common elements to fashion a lifeless human body but gave it vitality by breathing into it the "breath of life." Was the writer of Genesis 2 describing filling the body with breathable nitrogen and oxygen? Was he speaking of a mechanical process? What was he saying? What does this mean to you?

(2)   After using the hymn below ("Breathe On Me, Breath of God") as a prayer, compare its text to the above scripture.

Questions and suggestions based on the text

Day 1: pp. 30-36

a.   Begin listing the primary words you use in your own Expressive Prayers. As the days go by, make another column of affirmative, receptive terms that could also be used in these prayers. Notice when it is appropriate and helpful to pray with these latter terms.

b. What differences do you see between Receptive Prayer and a meditation which omits the essential ingredients listed on p. 31? Do these differences matter to you? Why or why not?

c. Would you like to learn more about any of the ways of using meditation mentioned on pp. 31 and 32? If so, which ones?

d. Comment on the statement on p. 33. "The one who prays accepts the *responsibility of being part of the answering process.*"

e. Do you agree or disagree with the statement on p. 33: "All healing (whether of relationships, spirit, mind, or body) is a removal of blockages, of hindrances or distractions..."? Give examples to support your response.

f. How can Receptive Prayer integrate an individual? Please note what Carl Jung says about awareness of conscious and unconscious responses.

Day 2: pp. 36-39

a. If it is true that "all of us meditate," can you think of instances when you did so, whether you intended to or not?

b. How do you respond to the idea that "Receptive Prayer (in its simplest form) is consciously being with God?"

c. The author points out the central, primary importance of prayerful receptivity in the lives of the prophets, Mary, outstanding spiritual leaders throughout history, and in the life of Jesus. She indicates that their ministry was built upon this receptivity and would not have been possible without it. Does this give you any new insights? What could you add to what she has written?

Day 3: pp. 40-43

a. On pp. 42 and 43 does the author "put down" speaking and asking in prayer or does she add more to prayer? What other statements on earlier pages support your answer?

b. Can you see how the forms or techniques of meditation could have been adopted by many for their *own* uses without the desire to open to God's will, guidance, and teaching? What do you think of my friend, Garth Thompson's play on some famous words: "Ask not what God can do for you, but what you can do for God?"

c. What do you know about other forms of meditation? Does your information come from a primary source, that is, from those who practice it? Perhaps you will want to make some notes comparing anything unique in tone, manner or purpose. If such notes are continued for a period of time, they can become a valuable reference.

d. Have you had any experiences which others would have considered extraordinary? Did they seem normal to you or special?

e. Many people are wary of experiential religion, fearing that people will seek emotional "kicks" rather than truth. What do you think?

f. Can one experience the presence of God in others? In themselves? In worship? What are the blessings or problems of such experiences?

g. If God were only outside us, and never in us, what good could God do?

h. Compare Romans 8: 26 and 27 with p. 42, especially the summary statement: "Prayer is not only toward God but from God."

Day 4: pp. 43-46

a. How do you respond to the statement: "Prayer can be detrimental or unhelpful?" Does this shock or surprise you? Do you agree or disagree? Why?

b. Can prayer increase either our sense of sinfulness or worth? Can it both harm and heal? Can it reveal what needs to be changed within us as well as give us strength to change?

    c.   Does it make sense to say: "The answer to Expressive Prayer may be in Receptive Prayer?"

    d.   What knowledge do you have of the workings of the brain that is useful here?

Day 5: pp. 46-49 through Section E

    a.   In this list of more than thirty ways of Receptive Prayer, note those which you feel you have already experienced (perhaps stating when and where), those you would like to develop, and those about which you have questions.

Day 6: Bottom of pp. 49 -51

    a.   There are always changes occurring in the Church. Do you feel that studying, teaching, and using Receptive Prayer could benefit the Church? Please support your response.

b. Is it possible that individual members could become more receptive to the presence of the Holy Spirit and more capable of listening to each other and to God in each other? How could this come about?

c. Sometimes life seems hopeless. Is there anything here which gives you hope?

Day 7: p. 52

a. Respond to p. 52 in terms of your own life experiences and understanding. Would you explain these passages any differently?

Hymns:
"Breathe On Me, Breath of God"
"Spirit of God" from the collection, *Joy Is Like the Rain.*
Sr. Miriam Therese Winter. New York, NY; Vangard Music Corp., 1965.

Memorization:

(1) Basic Format for Receptive Prayer on p. 31 paragraph 1.

(2) One stanza of the hymn may be learned each day or so. (The suggested text reads, in stanza three or four is: *"Til I am wholly Thine"* rather than "Unite my soul with Thine.")

QUIET RECEPTIVE PRAYER: *Breathing As a Way of Receiving*

A. Your breathing can be a powerful, physical reminder of releasing all of your life to God and receiving God's life in a continuous, habitual never-ending pattern. The pattern may be used in several ways: to release tension, pain, anger, or blockages, etc., as you exhale; then to welcome and claim God's presence, peace, life, or love as you inhale. The exhalation may also be used as self-dedication. Several ways are given below. When sharing Receptive Prayer with someone who has never done it, this is an excellent way to begin and is easy to explain.

Please refer to Section 2, A, B, and C on p. 145 of the text.

B. Instead of using Section A, you may use the Guided Prayer: "The Breath of God" on pp. 135 to 138 of the text.

ACTIVE RECEPTIVE PRAYER: *Bits and Breaths of Refreshment*

During the day, allow yourself tiny periods of refreshment. You can release tension quickly and easily by allowing your eyes to rest back in your head, your chin to loosen and chest to drop, and your hands to be relaxed and at rest, upturned on your lap. Take a few slow, deep breaths and drink in peace, love, or energy, realizing that each is a manifestation of God's continuous presence.

SECTION THREE

SEEING

Scripture reading:

Isaiah 6: 1-8, "Isaiah's Vision"

Questions based on the reading:

(1)   Describe, as well as you can, Isaiah's visionary experience.

(2)   Why was Isaiah so overwhelmed? Why was he so conscious of sin?

(3)   What freed him from disabling guilt and inspired him to offer his life?

(4)   Consider how this scripture relates to the hymn texts below. Then you may wish to use one of them as a prayer.

Questions based on the text:

Day 1: pp. 53-58 through the diagram

      a. How would you define "the Kingdom?" According to p. 54, how can you begin to receive it?

b. The story of the Prodigal Son (Luke 15: 11-32) in verse 17 uses the phrase: "When he came to himself..." What is "coming to ourselves?" What keeps us from it? What facilitates it?

c. Many of us pray for God to "make" things happen. Do you think that God works this way?

d. According to the author, what is the fundamental answer to all prayer?

e. Again, according to the author, what is the highest use of prayer? Why does the author use this terminology? Compare p. 42 with p. 54.

f. What is your response to the story of George Washington Carver?

g. Can you see any difference at this point between sleeping, merely resting, dreaming, daydreaming and Receptive Prayer?

h. How can you increase your energy at the end of a time of Receptive Prayer?

Day 2: pp. 58-62 through the diagram

a. Have you tried any of the ways of Simple Receptive Prayer suggested on pp. 58 to 62 and p. 145 to 148 or any of your own choosing? Are they effective? Do you have any questions about them? (Note that Simple Receptive Prayer requires no intentional relaxing since the focusing enables relaxing simultaneously.)

b. Do you have an opportunity to apply the ideas for using Receptive Prayer with children? How would you (or do you) proceed?

c. How do the first essentials of Receptive Prayer mentioned on p. 61 compare with the format memorized from p. 31 and repeated on p. 62?

Day 3: pp. 62 to middle of 69

a. What are the key words for Expanded Receptive Prayer?

b.   Would it be helpful to reassess your commitment to Quiet Receptive Prayer at this point? Have you chosen the best periods of the day and a useful amount of time?

What have you learned about avoiding disturbance or adjusting to it? What posture(s) do you find helpful?

c.   How do you respond to each of the sections on release? (Note especially the release of others, the past, and the future.)

d.   Why is dedication of the will so important?

e.   Why does release continue throughout Receptive Prayer?

Day 4: pp. 69-74

a.   Which of the ways of relaxing, focusing, and receiving have been or might be most useful to you?

b.   What do you think of the author's suggestion to those who are being prayed for by others: "to stop several times a day in order to receive what is being asked for in so many prayers?" (Note p. 76, paragraph 2, as well.)

    c.   Which statements in the "Receive" section are most meaningful to you? How do they compare to your own experiences or to those about which you have read?

Day 5: p. 75

    a.   Compare the sections entitled "Radiate" with pp. 37, 47 and lines 18 to 21 on p. 75. Is it clear to you how our normal spoken intercession for others can be effectively replaced by this step in Receptive Prayer?

    b.   What is different in these two ways of considering others in prayer? Do you feel that either would enable you to be a more effective channel for God's grace?

Day 6: pp. 75, 76 (Note last paragraph on p. 86 as well.)

    a.   Have you ever thought of forgiving yourself? What difference would it make? Does lack of self-forgiveness keep you from being what you want to be? What enables a person to forgive him or herself? (You will probably want to use your spiritual journal to write about this section adequately.)

b.   Are you more forgiving of others than of yourself? Vice versa? What does one have to do with the other?

c.   If each person is equally loved by God, what does this have to do with forgiveness of self or others?

d.   Will you _allow_ God to forgive you?   If you will allow God to forgive you in heaven, why not on earth?   Is God the Life-Giver?

e.   How can Receptive Prayer help you to claim the ability to forgive yourself and others and to let go of the pain of the past?

f.   How is forgiveness a kind of release? What does forgiveness have to do with healing?

g.   How can forgiveness go beyond itself to become blessing? How is this related to Jesus' words: "Pray for those who despitefully use you"? No one naturally wants to do this. Does it make sense to pray first that we learn to _want_ to bless them? Can someone begin to bless another who hurt them a long time ago?

h. What are the things you most want to remember regarding the use of Receptive Prayer in healing? Can you suggest some other effective procedures?

Day 7: pp. 76-80

a. Why is it important to remember what happened in Quiet Receptive Prayer?

b. Why is it important to return to normal functioning?

c. Why does the author suggest using reason to understand, assess, and follow through on the results of Receptive Prayer?

d. The most valid rational tests of the results of Receptive Prayer are the increased abilities to love and to be united with one's self and with others. How do you feel about applying these criteria to your own experience?

e. At this point in your use of Receptive Prayer, do you feel
    any difference in you attitudes or ideas, understanding,
    sense of worth, or ability to love?   Has anything
    changed?

f. What actions have you taken as a result of Receptive
    Prayer so far?

g. What is your present understanding of *Active* Receptive
    Prayer as mentioned, so far, on pp. 37, 49, and 78?

h. Why does the author say that Receptive Prayer "is not
    climbing to God?"   Why is meditation sometimes
    understood as an attempt to do this? What does Martin
    Luther's following explanation of the third article of the
    Apostle's Creed have to do with this question: *"I believe
    that I cannot, by my own reason or strength, believe in
    Jesus Christ, my Lord, or come to him*; but the Holy
    Ghost has called me... enlightened..., and sanctified
    me..."? What is your response to Luther's statement in
    the light of Receptive Prayer?

i. How do you feel about "spiritual report cards" for
    yourself and others in regard to progress in Receptive
    Prayer?

Hymns:

"My God, How Wonderful Thou Art" (stanzas 1, 3, and 5.)
"Be Thou My Vision, O Lord of My Heart" (stanza 1)
"Teach Me, My God and King, in All Things Thee to See"
(all stanzas)

Memorization:

(1) The first stanza of "Teach Me, My God and King"
(2) John 14: 20
(3) The first three sentences of p. 80.

QUIET RECEPTIVE PRAYER: *Visualization As a Way of Receiving*

Read *The Light of Life*, the Guided Receptive Prayer on pp. 136 to 141. It will give you an idea of the pattern of the Receptive Prayer to be followed. You may slowly and clearly read these words into a tape recorder and use the recording thereafter. Portions of it may be omitted if the main emphases are retained. *Otherwise* you may follow these suggestions:

Relax your body and dedicate your will to God. Then visualize God's light surrounding and filling you to overflowing.

When you are ready, bring to mind someone whom you love, visualizing them as being surrounded and filled with this same light which blesses, heals, and enlightens them.

Then bring to mind someone who has hurt or harmed you. See that person surrounded and filled by this same light, just as your loved one was. Realizing that you are seeing this person in God's light, allow yourself to look at him or her in a

44

new way, imagining that you are looking "with God's eyes" and understanding as God would understand. Give yourself time.

Remember what has happened.

Return to the present.

Write in your spiritual journal anything you wish to remember, mentioning any insight or experience of worth, or any inspiration that has come to you.

Mentally review the day and days ahead considering people and projects with whom you will be involved. Make a note of what you wish to do or good ideas as to how to proceed. Then move to Active Receptive Prayer.

ACTIVE RECEPTIVE PRAYER: *Looking for God in Life*

Throughout the days ahead:

(1) Look for God's beauty and grace in all living things and in the work of people's hands and minds.

(2) Visualize goals for yourself and society clearly, bravely, and in a practical way, holding to that visualization until you replace it with a better one.

SECTION FOUR

LISTENING

Scripture reading:

> I Kings 19: 1-13, "The Still, Small Voice"
>
> John 12: 23-30, "The Voice That Thundered"

Questions based on the reading:

(1) What do you know about the Prophet Elijah, about his challenges, strengths, and weaknesses?

(2) About what situation does this particular wilderness story tell?

(3) In your opinion, what part did trust play in the life of Elijah?

(4) What do verses 11-13 mean to you? Various translations say: "the sound of a gentle breeze," "a murmuring sound," and "a voice of silence."

(5) Do you feel that God has communicated with you? In what ways? Have you ever received interior guidance through

words which could not be heard by the ears but were thought or heard in the brain? Do you know of cases where someone you admire or trust has had such an experience?

(6) Please read the following passage from St. Augustine's *Confessions*, Chap. X. (trans. C. Bigg, London: Metheun & Co., 1929)

"If the tumult of the flesh were hushed; hushed these shadows of earth, sea, sky; hushed the heavens and the soul itself; if all dreams were hushed, and all sensuous revelations, and every tongue and every symbol; if all that comes and goes were hushed – They all proclaim to him that hath an ear: 'We made not ourselves: he made us who abideth for ever' – But suppose that, having delivered their message, they held their peace, turning their ear to Him who made them, and that He alone spoke, not by them but for Himself, and we heard His word, not by any fleshly tongue, nor by an angel's voice, nor in the thunder, nor in any similitude, but His voice whom we love in these His creatures – Suppose we heard Him without any intermediary at all – Just now we reached out, and with one flash of thought touched the Eternal Wisdom that abides above all – Suppose this endured, and all other far inferior modes of vision were taken away, and this alone were to ravish the beholder, and absorb him, and plunge him into mystic joy, might not eternal life be like this moment of comprehension for which we sighed? Is not this the meaning of 'Enter thou into the joy of thy Lord?' Ah, when shall this be? Shall it be when 'we all rise, but shall not all be changed'?"

(7) If and when God speaks, do you think it is always in "a still, small voice?" Can you support this with scripture or other writings? *After* thinking about this, note John 12: 23-30.

(8) Compare this I Kings passage with the severe testing of Jesus in the wilderness. (Matthew 4: 1-11)

(9) How do these words strike you: "What are you doing here, Elijah?"? Notice that they are repeated. Why did Elijah need to be asked?

(10) Have you ever felt that God was asking you the same question?

(11) Compare the hymns below with the above scripture.

Questions based on the text

Day 1: pp. 80-83

    a.   According to the author, what was the outstanding characteristic of the life of Jesus? How can it be said that his life was one of continuous Receptive Prayer?

    b.   What makes a meditation Christian? How does Christian meditation compare with other types of meditation? What are the similarities or differences?

    c.   Do you see the purpose of this text as a "put down" of other forms of meditation, as an exultation of the Christian way, or as a means to know and understand Christian traditions and concepts in meditation?

    d.   Do you believe that the *core* of meditation, which is the experience of the holy and the transcendent, is similar or different for those using other forms of meditation? Is there value to you in learning from others who meditate what their practice and experience is?

Day 2: p. 83.

> a. Do you think that Receptive Prayer will make you more self-centered or more directed toward others? Do you think it already has made you more sensitive to others, more loving, and/or more helpful? Please explain.

> b. Do you find yourself habitually remembering others during your time of Receptive Prayer? If so, has this affected your relationship with them or your understanding of them? *Do you include those who frustrate you or those who bless you* or both?

Day 3: pp. 84 and 85 to "faith"

> a. How would you define repentance? What does it have to do with one's direction in life?

> b. How would you define detachment? What does it have to do with letting go? With allowing freedom? With destruction? With respect?

> c. How are repentance and detachment similar to each other, and how are they different?

d. What do they have to do with Receptive Prayer?

Day 4: pp. 85-87

    a. How would you compare faith with grace?

    b. How would you compare trust with responsibility?

    c. We are often exhorted to "just trust God and he will take care of us;" does this mean that we need bear no responsibility nor exercise any effort?

    d. How are both grace and faith involved in Receptive Prayer?

Day 5: pp. 87-88

    a. How are repentance and detachment, self-denial and renunciation like dying?

    b. What does the author mean by saying: "We die in order to be reborn?" (p. 88)

c. What does the Crucifixion teach us about our living and our praying?

d. According to the author, what is the most important point in Receptive Prayer? Do you think that this point is ever reached? Partially? Completely? By whom? Briefly? Permanently?

e. Give your understanding of Galatians 2: 20: "I have been crucified with Christ. It is no longer I who live, but Christ who lives in me; the life I now live...I live by faith in the Son of God." (*This is an extremely important understanding. If it is new to you, please give yourself time to begin to comprehend it.*)

f. How does Receptive Prayer relate to or reflect Galatians 2: 20?

Day 6: pp. 88-91

a. What differences or similarities do you see in the viewpoint toward the self in Christian meditation versus that of others?

b. What do you think it means to be, as the Apostle Paul said: "God's temple," "God's field," " God's building?"

c. Is it possible for you to see yourself or others this way?

Day 7: pp. 91 to mid 93

a. Do you perceive the body as a hindrance to the spirit or as an agent of the spirit? Can it be both or either? Explain.

b. What does the author mean by saying: "Nothing we think we possess is really our own."?

Hymns:

. "Here I Am, Lord"
"I Will Come to You in the Silence"
"Mid All the Traffic of the Ways"
"O Little Town of Bethlehem"
("How silently ... the wondrous Gift is giv'n.... Where meek souls will receive Him, *still*...") (author's emphasis)

If you wish, use hymns as spoken or mental (thought) prayers now and in the following days.

Memorization:

> (1)   A review of the Basic Format on p. 62.

> (2)   Memorization of the eight steps of Expanded Receptive Prayer on the bottom of p. 63. (Important)

> (3)   Perhaps one stanza of one of the preceding hymns.

GUIDED RECEPTIVE PRAYER: *Listening As a Way of Receiving*

Begin by thinking of the words of the "Lord of Love" prayer on p. 29. They will express the offering of your will and your relaxation in trust.

Let them lead you into further rest and trust,
> into knowing that your life is in God's hands
> and you are completely his.

Let the words be your dedication of all you have and are,
> and let them mold you into yieldedness,
> ready to receive.

Then look up, at, into, and through the place
> upon which your gaze is resting,
> and gently close your eyes.

Listen to all the sounds around you.
> If there are many, listen to all of them as a whole,
> knowing that each is part of the whole,
> that all are bound together.....

> (If you were in space you would realize that all the

sounds of the world are engulfed in one great silence.)

Then begin to listen for the quieter sounds among them,
        and for the most constant sound,
        like a thread running through it all:
        it may be high or low, or sounded in a chord
        inaudible except in moments like these.

Move your attention then to listen to the sounds within you.
        If, at first, you discover none,
        Listen to the silence. Savor it.
        Let it feed you and bless you.

Know that that silence echoes within your deepest self,
        that there is a space within you
        that rests in perfect peace,
        that rests in God.....

Perhaps you will eventually hear
        the faintest of vibrations.

If that is true, let them remind you of that part of life
        of which we are usually unaware, that dimension
        which is more real and more constant
        than the changing world around us.

Do not strain. Do not try to hear. Do not demand.

Listen to whatever is found in your deepest self,
        whether sound or silence,
        and let it speak to you of God
        for as long as you wish.

Let it remind you that God is not only in the outside world,
        but deep within the world and you,

that there is no time or place
where God cannot be found.

Stay in that knowing ....
....

Before you leave the silence,
think of someone whom you want to bless:
a loved one or a so-called "antagonist,"
a world leader or someone with great responsibilities;
a stranger in need or a forgotten soul
whom no one knows:
the beggar you saw on the street,
a nameless prisoner in an unknown prison,
an abandoned child somewhere..... ,
and let your mind bring them into this reservoir of
peace..................
....

You will ask, as well, if there is anything else
you should bring to mind....

Then you will remember all that you want to take with you
or return to again....

Come back gradually...., gently....., fully... completely.
Listen... See... Hear... Feel.... Stretch all over.....
Breathe deeply and let the energy build! ....
You are in the present! ....
You are rested..., refreshed..., at peace.

Now you will review the day ahead of you,
noting what is important to do,
things that otherwise would have been
forgotten or unconsidered,

thinking of relationships that may be made,
writing down what should not be forgotten,
and noting new insights, or perspectives
in your spiritual journal.....
Take your time........

Now you will move to respond to the world around you through Active Receptive Prayer.

ACTIVE RECEPTIVE PRAYER: Listening for God in Life
Learning to live receptively through listening:
to God in the peace of silence,
to expressions of God's life in and through music,
to God's guidance when it is in the words of others,
and listening to others, themselves, with compassion,
understanding, and discernment,
by endeavoring to hear not only words and tone
of voice, but what they mean to say.

SECTION FIVE

AFFIRMING

Scripture readings:

I Samuel 3: 1-10 - "God's Call and Affirmation of Samuel"

Exodus 3: 1-14 and 4: 10-16 – "God's Call and Affirmation of Moses"

Questions based on the first reading: I Samuel 3: 1-10

(1) What do these words mean: "The word of the Lord was rare in those days; there was no frequent vision."?

(2) The ark of God was considered by the Israelites to be the dwelling place of God's presence, and the burning lamp symbolizing God's presence had not yet gone out as the little boy Samuel lay near them, quiet, but not yet asleep. What influence may his surroundings have had on him?

(3) What do you think verse 7 means: "Samuel did not yet know the Lord and the word of the Lord had not yet been revealed to him."?

(4) What do you think was happening in this story?

(5)   Compare this story with the first hymn below.

Questions based on the second reading:

Exodus 3: 1-14 and 4: 10-16

(1)   How did Moses feel and what did his words mean when he said: "Who am I that I should go to Pharaoh and bring the sons of Israel out of Egypt?"

(2)   God spoke to Moses so that Moses could speak for him. What do you think of Exodus 4: 10-16? What do you think of Moses? Do you identify with him at all? Are you glad there was an Aaron? Do you wish that the story had been different in any way?

(3)   Does this story say anything to you about your own speaking?

(4)   Compare these passages with the second hymn below.

Questions based on the text

Day 1: pp. mid. 93-top 97

      a.   In your own words, how would you define: repeated affirmation, *hesychasm, mantra* and song word?

      b.   How is God's call an affirmation of a human being?

      c.   How do we affirm God in prayer?

      d.   What would you say (or sing or think) as a sincere affirmation from your own heart?

Day 2: pp. 97 - mid. 98

      a.   What are the problems with repetition in worship?

      b.   What are the values of repetition in worship?

c. Why has repetition been used so universally by various religions?

d. What do you think of the author's explanation of Matthew 6: 7?

Day 3: pp. mid. 98 – mid. 99

a. Do we pray according to what we have been taught or according to the way we feel? Are they necessarily the same?

b. Which is more honest and helpful in your view?

Day 4: pp. 99-101

a. Have you ever studied or practiced meditation before using Receptive Prayer? If so, how has your previous experience affected your understanding and use of Receptive Prayer?

b. How has the study and practice of Receptive Prayer affected your previous concepts and attitudes toward meditation?

Day 5: pp. 101-mid. 104

    a.   What do you see as misuses of meditation?

    b.   How much should a person withdraw from the world? If withdrawal is appropriate or necessary, when is that true?

    c.   How much should one be involved in the world?

    d.   Are people, such as monks and nuns who live in seclusion, of any help to society?

    e.   On the other side of the coin, have you ever become so busy doing God's work that you lost contact with God?

Day 6: pp. 104-107

    a.   What do you think of the statement regarding Jesus' forty days in the wilderness: "His previous forty spent listening to his Father had not kept him from temptation but had prepared him for it and guided him through it."?

b. If the above is true, what can we expect of our own listening for and to God?

c. Is it true that those who are close to God (i.e., receptive to God) do not have any problems?...or could grow beyond them?...or always rise above them?...or live with and in spite of them?

d. Could you describe in your own words the three life perspectives or pictures from which Jesus (and we) could choose, according to the author?

e. Would you like to add to, subtract from, or change these summary statements in any way? If so, how?

f. Do you think there is any danger of spiritual pride among people who have had some outstanding spiritual experiences? What difference does spiritual pride make?

g. Does the unifying presence of God end with a transfixed state or result in love in action? Meditators of various schools sometimes differ greatly on this point. How do you feel?

h. Why does the author emphasize incarnation so strongly?

i. What is your explanation of the relationship between the so-called sacred and secular, supernatural and natural, material and spiritual, eternal and temporal? Are they opposites? Is one inside the other? Is one an expression, an instrument or manifestation of the other?

j. Does Receptive Prayer put you in touch with one or both sides of these "pairs?"

k. On pp. 107 and 79, the author has pointedly stated: "All things are *distractions from God* until all things become *expressions of God.*"

How do you understand this? Do you agree? Could a distraction become an expression, or vice versa? How?

Day 7: pp. bottom 107-109

a. What do you think of the statements:

"Eternal life is the most real thing that exists. When we are unaware of it for long we are sick."?

b. How do you explain John 17: 2,3:

"And this is eternal life, that men should know thee, the only true God and Jesus Christ whom thou hast sent."?

c. What causes one to miss "the great and wonderful Gift?"

d. Page 109 reads: "The test of *Quiet* Receptive Prayer is..." What is this test?

Hymns: (See Hymn Sources for more.)

"Alleluia" – p. 96 in text
"I Sought the Lord"
"Master, Speak! Thy Servant Hearest" (MH p. 274)
"Lord, Speak to Me That I May Speak"

I Sought the Lord

Unknown Poet

Grace Brame

I sought the Lord and af-ter-ward I knew... He mov'd my soul to seek Him seek-ing me. It was not I who found Thee Sav-ior true. No! I was found by Thee.

Memorization: (from "Lord, Speak to Me "):

"O fill me with Thy fulness, Lord,
  Until my very heart o'erflow
  In kindling thought and glowing word
  Thy love to tell, thy praise to show."

GUIDED RECEPTIVE PRAYER: *Affirmation as a Way of Receiving* (Many call this form "Centering Prayer.")

Choose an affirmation. It may well be:
        "All I am is yours and all you are is mine," or "Into Thy hands I commend my spirit," or "My Lord and my God!" or singing the "Alleluia" on p. 96 of the text.
Then,

Sitting in a comfortable position, allow your body and mind to become quiet.

Remember your affirmation. Say or sing it aloud several times,
        meaning it
        and hearing it.

Then hear it in your mind. At first you are remembering how you heard it with your ears. You are no longer making the effort to say it. You are simply hearing it mentally.

Over and over it is repeated and your mind is fastened on it as words and meaning become more deeply embedded in your spirit.

Perhaps it will change in some way: in rhythm or volume or intensity. You continue listening.

You may become distracted. That is no cause for alarm. Notice what has distracted you; then let it go, and merely return to your affirmation. Allow the distraction no added power by fastening on it or by feeling angry or guilty at its presence. Simply return to your affirmation for as long as you wish.

Eventually you will no longer hear the words, but their meaning, or the feeling you have derived from them, or the reality with which they have put you in touch will become the center of your attention.

On some days your experience will be deeper than others. This does not matter. What does matter is acknowledging that God is real, and knowing that you belong to incomprehensible Love, whether you feel it or not.

Accept whatever comes to you in the time you have set aside. Bring at least one other person to mind before you finish. Come back to the present gently and completely as you have before. Set down in your journal all that you would like to remember. Then proceed to Active Receptive Prayer.

ACTIVE RECEPTIVE PRAYER: Affirmation of God in Life

How often, and how genuinely, do you affirm others?

Aware that it is God who enables you to see and speak, attempt to look at others, yourself, and life as the Spirit of God directs, and then, by words and action, gaze and tone of voice, to express your affirmation of God's life in others whenever appropriate. Affirm in others their worth, their potential, and their meaning in your life. You do not need to be blind to that with which you disagree or that which seems to hinder their greatest good. In fact, if you do put on blinders, you will not be helpful. But you can look for, encourage, and bring forth their best whenever possible.

Notice especially those who are shy or who do not realize their capabilities. Notice those whose individual importance seems to be ignored. Notice those whom you might otherwise take for granted, especially the many whom you "expect" to be faithful, to "do their job." See what is special or unusual. Affirm those whose vision and strength empower others to be fulfilled. Affirm the compassionate and courageous with your support. Express your gratitude to those who are happy and bring the gift of their joy to others. Celebrate uniqueness and worth with your active affirmation. Notice how we help to make the people around us what they are. Notice how some people become what they think ... we think ... they are! It is an enormous privilege to help someone see the treasure that is in them.

SECTION SIX

TOUCHING

Scripture reading:

Jeremiah 18: 1-6

Questions based on the reading:

(1)   Why was it easier for Jeremiah to hear God at the potter's house?

(2)   Since the potter did not throw away the imperfect vessel but recreated it into a new and unspoiled container, what message did this bring to Jeremiah? What message does it bring to you?

(3)   It is easy to feel that we have wasted part of our lives or talents or even our love. Is it true or untrue that nothing is wasted? In what sense?

(4)   Is it possible for God to reclaim or remold us in Receptive Prayer?

(5)   Compare the scripture with the old hymn below: "Have Thine Own Way, Lord."

Questions based on the text

Day 1: pp. 110-mid. 112

    a.   What does the author see as the primary result of Receptive Prayer? Do you agree? What is your experience? Where is God? What difference does it make? Where and when and what is eternity?

    b.   How does one's understanding of the above affect the way one lives and dies?

    c.   Would your answers to the above be different on a happier day than today, or on a sadder day?

    d.   Are the answers based on what you think sometimes different from those based on what you experience or feel?

    e.   When God seems to be gone, what helps you?

    f.   What is the anchor to which you hold when life seems darkest or hardest? What thought, reality, book, person, truth, etc., is your anchor?   How does this affect your prayer?

Day 2: pp. 112-mid. 113

    a. What do you think is the difference between being spiritually asleep or awake?

    b. If changes occur during Receptive Prayer, who or what changes?

    c. What is the relationship between Receptive Prayer and the passages of Matthew 22: 32 and John 11: 26?

    d. How do you explain those two passages?

    e. Do you see how Receptive Prayer can be used to help the dying?

Day 3: pp. 113, 114

    a.   What does Receptive Prayer have to do with trusting? Can you explain trusting or give an example? Is it hard or easy? When and why?

    b.   What are the Fruits of the Spirit? Why are they so often overlooked in comparison to the Gifts of the Spirit?

    c.   What is *your* Spiritual Identity?

Day 4: p. 115

    a.   What are the gifts of the Spirit?

    b.   Do you think they should be ignored or used if given? If used, in what manner? (I Corinthians 12, 13 and 14 may be used as reference, especially 12: 7, 13: 13, and 14: 1a.)

    c.   In what sense is all healing spiritual, whether through doctors and medicine, counselors and attitude, friends and loving support, prayer, or the laying on of hands?

Day 5: p. 116

    a.   What unordinary experiences have come to you or others through Receptive Prayer?

    b.   How did you (or they) respond to these experiences? Were they useful or helpful?

    c.   What did they teach you?

Day 6: pp. 117 – top 118

    a.   How important are phenomena (such as unusual sights or sounds during prayer) in comparison to the realization of God's presence?

    b.   How important is it to evaluate Receptive Prayer by the standards of increased love, or unity with the world and within yourself? (This is a purposely repeated question.)

    c.   Do you think that visions or revelations might come to anyone in our time? Why or why not?

d. Is it possible or useful to attempt exact repetition of results of a meditative experience?

e. How do you feel about requiring signs from God?

Day 7: pp. 118- mid. 119

a. Has Receptive Prayer changed your consciousness, your sensitivities, your priorities, or your mission in life?

b. What great religious figures have had periods of darkness, weakness, or feeling forsaken even after times of tremendous accomplishment and spiritual fulfillment?

c. Using the quotation from Luther on p. 119, explain the meaning of sanctification.

d. What, to you, is the most important result of Receptive Prayer, the thing most to be treasured?

Hymns:

"Have Thine Own Way, Lord"
"Spirit of the Living God"
"O God, You Search Me and You Know Me" (GA2, p. 509) (See Psalm 139)
"Lord, Thou Hast Searched Me" (EH, p. 702)
"Amazing Grace"

Memorization: The hymn, "Spirit of the Living God," p. 13.

GUIDED RECEPTIVE PRAYER: *God's Healing Touch*

(The following Guided Receptive Prayer may be read into a tape recorder to be used, or read and remembered as well as possible. The primary things to remember are the Seven Steps of Extended Receptive Prayer and the Focus which is to see yourself as God's vessel, molded and filled by him. Your own hands are placed upon your body as a reminder of God's presence, touching you and recreating you in God's love.)

....

"Lie down comfortably on your back
on a clean carpet
or on a blanket on the floor
or on the earth if this is comfortable.
Be sure that the place and position of your body enhances,
but does not distract from your Receptive Prayer.

Let your weight melt into the floor (ground).....
from every part of your body.....

Offer your whole self to God:
body, mind, and spirit.
Do this wordlessly.....

or with some silent dedication
such as the prayer called "The Lord of Love"(Text, p. 29)

With this self-giving pervading you,
       look at a spot in the ceiling (or the sky).
       Look at it,....., into it.....,
       through it......, and beyond it.
       Then, still looking, close your eyelids.....

Someone once said, describing prayer:
       "I am looking at God,
       and God is looking at me."
       Receptive Prayer begins this way.....

As you have gazed into, and through,
       and beyond the point of
       focus with your eyes,
       your mind has begun to look at God,
       and you are aware that, as always,
       God is looking at you,
       looking at you in love,
       as a creator looks at the creator's handiwork
       and holds it in tender love.

Held there, within this care,
       you begin to see as the Creator sees.
       You see yourself as God's vessel
       made to hold God's love.....,
       a vessel sometimes filled with beauty,
       sometimes touched with pain, imperfect,
       sometimes broken open with remembered agony
       sometimes overflowing with the power and the presence
           of the God of love,
       but, potentially, a masterpiece,
       through the grace.....of the Artist/Craftsman.

"Who am I?" you ask.

    "Why am I here on earth?"

    And the One who made you says: "Dear child," then
        names your name so you can hear it.................

    "You are mine."

    "I have called you by name. You are *mine*."

Held there, you realize

    that God loves you as you are,
    and wants to make you more.
    Beyond what you ordinarily would see,
    God sees what you have the power to be,
    the potential placed in you
    at your very beginning.

In gratitude you listen,

    held profoundly close
    to the heart of God

God and you begin to pick up the broken pieces of your life!

Together you search for those that are so hard to find,

    the pieces you have purposely hidden away
    so that they would never be revealed
    to anyone,
    not even to yourself.

By this gentle, forgiving Spirit,

    the pieces of your life are gathered,
    then held in godly hands
    as God's beloved treasure,
    And God says: "It is *GOOD*!"

And you respond.

You offer yourself as clay
into the hands of the potter.
so that you may be molded
the pieces, even the imperfections,
are transforming into something new.

You have placed yourself into God's hands,
and now, you place your own hands
somewhere on your body,
letting them remind you
of God's own touch of blessing
and of healing.

Perhaps your hands will lie above your heart
as you open it to forgiveness and greater love.
.....

Perhaps your palms will rest upon your lips
as you remember how your words
can harm or heal.
.....

Perhaps your hands will lie
upon a place of pain
where God's love now flows
to bring you peace,
to open dark, tight places
which soak in
light and energy: the Creator's life!.....

And if you are too tired to hold your hands there for a while,
Let them lie at rest upon your solar plexus
and see God's hands upon the places
where the need is greatest.

You let the Creator create.....
      Silently.....
      Wonderfully.....

You are being melted.....
      molded.....
      filled.....

Your heart in joyous receptivity
      sings and sings
      "O fill me in you fullness Lord,
      until my very heart o'erflow,
      in kindling thought and glowing word,
      Your to tell,
      Your praise to show." *

Here is the Potter who never throws away
      any precious vessel,
      but takes each one as it is,
      and with a recreating touch of love,
      fashions it anew!

You yield completely!

And your yielding is your joy!

The One who first gave you life
      will make you into
      a chalice of the Spirit
      and fill you with God's love!...................

From now on, you can do nothing but tell others of such love,
      and share it wherever you go

Now it is time to remember what has happened
in your body, mind, and heart.

As a vessel full of blessing
there is more than enough to share!
Mentally bring some other one
to be touched and filled
as you have been.................

Now think of those whom you will soon meet,
those with whom you will share
the contents of the chalice of your life.
See that meeting as it can be,
in God's grace.....

Then, stretching and breathing deeply,
gradually and gently return
to the time and place around you.

Write down all that you would remember.
Note new plans and possibilities
and fresh under-standings.

Then begin to *live*
in Active Receptive Prayer.

* From "Take My Life and Let It Be Consecrated"

ACTIVE RECEPTIVE PRAYER: *Touching for God in Life*

Knowing that *"God is at work in you,* both *to will* and *to work*
for *his good pleasure"* (Philippians 2: 13), claim the
power of the Holy within you. See yourself as the vessel
out of which God's love is to be poured. Remind yourself
to open so that the Holy Spirit may fill you, flow from

you, and touch others intentionally for God, so that all the work you do will be done by the Holy Spirit in you. God has no hands but ours to bless, to heal, to do God's work. You may keep in your mind the thought: "May all I touch with my mind, my gaze, or my hands, be touched by God in me."

SECTION SEVEN

LOVING

Scripture Readings for the Week:
> Jeremiah 1: 4-8;
> John 15: 4, 5, and 16; and
> Psalm 139: 1-18.

Questions based on the Scripture:

(1)   According to Jeremiah 1: 5, God called Jeremiah to be his own even before he was conceived. Does this speak to you personally?

(2)   According to the end of verse 5, God gave Jeremiah a particular task to do. Do you feel you have been given any particular task or any particular way of doing your daily work?

(3)   Jeremiah was, in the vernacular, "scared" at God's call. "I'm only a kid!" he said. How does this parallel some of the challenges and feelings in your own life? Do you feel called to do something and want to do it, yet feel afraid because of inadequacy? *What could you do if you were not afraid?* Please be sure to answer this.

(4)   Do you think that learning to receive could take time? How much? A lifetime?

(5)   Note the similarity between the Lord touching Jeremiah's mouth and Isaiah's visionary angel touching his lips. Both men felt overwhelmingly inadequate: Isaiah because of sin and Jeremiah because of lack of experience. What was given to Isaiah (Chapter 6: 1-8) and to Jeremiah to enable them to proceed? Did they receive what was given?

(6)   Is there any way in which God speaks to you, personally, through these passages?

(7)   How does John 15: 16, where Jesus is talking to the disciples, relate to the stories of Mary, Samuel, Isaiah, and Jeremiah? How does it relate to you? How does it relate to verses 4 and 5?

(8)   What is "abiding?"

(9)   Compare verses 4 and 5 with John 14: 16, 17, and 20.

(10) What do the above verses have to do with Receptive Prayer?

(11) How does Psalm 139: 1-18 relate to the Jeremiah story? What does it have to do with abiding? ... and Receptive Prayer?

(12) Comment, as you wish, on the hymns and memory selections.

Questions based on the text

Day 1: End p. 119-120

a. Is it self-centered to seek to know ourselves through Receptive Prayer? Might it be dangerous for ourselves and others *not* to know ourselves?

b. What good can we do others by knowing ourselves?

Day 2: End p. 120-123

a. How would you define "doing theology?"

b. What is the obvious theme of Active Receptive Prayer? How does this theme compare to the lifetime response of Mary and the Prophets?

c. Do you think that God "makes" things happen? How will the answer to this question affect our prayers?

d. How can we do the works of Christ and greater as noted in John 14: 12, 16, 17, and 26?

e. What does "Thy Kingdom come" have to do with Receptive Prayer? What does it have to do with the earth as a vessel for God's spirit?

f. What do you see as the difference between being spiritually perceptive but psychologically naïve? What does it mean to be "heavenly minded but no earthly good?"

Day 3: pp. 123-125

a. What enables Receptive Prayer to be a channel for healing?

b. Do the stories on pp. 122 and 123 compare with any of your own? Do they encourage you to use Receptive Prayer for healing of the *whole* person (not just physical problems) in group meetings or church services? If, in our prayers, we petition for healing at these gatherings, can we also be open to receiving it and taking time to be healed?

c. How does Receptive Prayer unite us with others? Have you had such experiences personally? Did they affect your subsequent relationships or actions?

Day 4: End of pp. 125-127

a. What is your reaction to the last paragraph on p. 125? Do you agree or disagree?

b. What is it about Receptive Prayer that enables one to endure *or* to let go of problems, people, or life? Do you perceive letting go and giving up as identical or different? Are they (or which is) positive or negative? creative or defeating?

c. Which of the results mentioned on the bottom of p. 127 have been part of your experience in Receptive Prayer? Can you understand others for whom the results have been different?

d. How could you use Receptive Prayer in preparation for a specific task or activity? Which?

Day 5: End of p. 127 – mid. 129

a. How would you write the last paragraph on p. 127 (on inner change) in your own words? How do you feel about it?

b. What does the Spirit of God have to do with Receptive Prayer?

c. What does Romans 12: 2 (top p. 128) mean to you?

d. How can anyone in the midst of pain or awesome challenge, truthfully and unhypocritically say: "I shall not want" and really feel that way? Have you ever had that kind of experience?

e. Specifically how could Receptive Prayer be used in your church? Choose one of the following to consider:

worship services; retreats; council meetings; Sunday School; choir; youth groups; circles; prayer groups, healing, or study groups; therapy groups; or with the sick or counselees? (The author's book, "Living Together in Prayer," yet to be published, deals exclusively with this question.)

Day 6: pp. 129-131

    a. Why does the author combine "knowing God" and loving? How are they similar?

    b. Please list the possible gifts that could be given through Receptive Prayer. Include what you have already received.

    c. What does the author indicate as "the greatest gain in all our searching"?

    d. Compare Questions b and c with I Cor. 13.

    e. What do you see as the main point in Augustine's words quoted on p. 130?

    f. Comment, as you wish, on the memory selections from p. 130-131 (noted below).

Day 7: pp. 132-135

a. What do you think are the most important qualifications of one who leads Guided Receptive Prayer? How important is experience in Receptive Prayer? ... sensitivity to text ... audibility of the voice? ... a sense of pacing? How would one prepare?

b. Now that you have read the book, what is your response to this basic question: "If God is always answering prayer, but we do not receive, what good does it do to pray?"

c. Note Isaiah 65: 24: "Before they call I will answer, while they are yet speaking I will hear." Do you believe this is true? If so, what good will yielding, self-offering, focusing, waiting, and trusting, all aspects of receiving, do?

d. What questions or convictions do you have as a result of this course? How do you plan to act on them?

e. What parts of "The Shepherd Psalm" mean the most to you? How/Why?

Hymns:

"O Love That Will Not Let Me Go"
"You Satisfy the Hungry Heart" (if there is a final Communion)
"On Eagle's Wings"
"I Sought the Lord"
"Go, My Children, With My Blessing"

Memorization: Jeremiah 1: 5 and John 1: 12 or Verse 1 of *I Sought the Lord*

QUIET RECEPTIVE PRAYER: *Loving God and Letting God Love You* or *The Shepherd Psalm, p. 133, Text.*

Loving God and letting God love you is a form of Simple Receptive Prayer. It can be done sitting, lying on your back, or walking in a quiet, beautiful place. If you walk, it should be somewhere where you can bask in the sunshine or immerse yourself in the sky. It is not wise to walk where you will meet other people or animals, where what you see distracts your mind, or where the surface is uneven so that you may fall.

Simple Receptive Prayer is the bedrock of living receptively. It is natural and uncomplicated. Yet knowing how to relax, choosing the spirit of self-offering, and having a habit of focusing is helpful if distractions or stress is present. On the whole, the actual content of Simple Receptive Prayer naturally evokes relaxation, self-offering, and focus. If needed, you may reread pages 58-62. You may want to say or sing aloud at first: "I love you God. And you love me!" Do not continue to listen to those words for long. Go beyond the words to just loving and being loved.

Loving God and letting God love you will at first be offering and receiving. Eventually, however, these will melt together and you will be aware only of Love itself beyond all giving and receiving.

ACTIVE RECEPTIVE PRAYER: *Loving God in Life*

BENEDICTION AND COMMISSION:

"You are deeply loved. It is God who claims you, your life, your words, and your work. All of these are the action of God's spirit alive in you. Thus your words ..., deeds ..., ...touch, and the look in your eyes and your smile will become God's outreaching to those you are led to bless. So live your life that *living* will be your way of *loving* God. So live your life that *living* will be your way of *loving* God.

"This is our prayer:

'Lord, be the life of my life, so that all I do may be what you do through me.'"

(P. 136 *Faith, the Yes of the Heart*, Brame)

91

FROM HERE ON:

CONTINUED PRACTICE AND STUDY

What you have experienced through this book is only a beginning. Another book may someday take us further on this journey together. But there is much that you can do on your own with the materials at hand or available elsewhere. Now you are probably at a very special place. You have established some habits which have been beneficial in a number of ways. In order to build upon what you have gained, you will want to keep and reinforce these habits. Here are some ways in which you can do this:

(1)   It is important to continue the practice of Quiet Receptive Prayer. You may have found one way which is especially right for you. If so, you may want to continue that for months or years as the process becomes more and more an effective channel for God to use. Others may feel comfortable in exploring other ways. Many are noted in the textbook. Each has its own gift to give. In the end, however, the exploration is not the important thing, and being a dilettante about methods could keep you from learning any method well. Deepening your ability to receive is what matters.

Note: Many people prefer to use *lectio divina* followed by some other form of Receptive Prayer.

(2)   Many books and courses on the subject of meditation, in general, are available, and a number of excellent books about Christian meditation, in particular, are published. Knowing what others have to say will enlarge and sharpen your understanding tremendously. The text you have just read, while it goes far beyond fundamentals, has purposely pointed out the essentials as seen by the author. It should form a good foundation upon which to gain more information and practice. For further assistance, note the bibliography.

(3) Scripture reading can continue to undergird your Receptive Prayer. If you have a concordance, look up all references to key words in Receptive Prayer such as: "Listen," "hear," "see," "perceive," "wait," "trust," and "rest." As you listen to the reading of scripture in church services or elsewhere be aware of themes to which you want to return.

(4) Buy one or two hymnals or songbooks for yourself. Continue to use hymns as part of your devotions and as a resource for some of the finest material to memorize.

(5) You may want to try posting a passage to be memorized, a Thought for the Week, or *your own* new approach to Active Receptive Prayer. Choose a place which you frequently pass: a bulletin board, a door, a refrigerator, or a mirror. You may also write the words on a card to slip into a wallet or purse or post on the dashboard of your car. Be sure to change these so that you will not take them for granted!

(6) Perhaps you may want to continue this group or form several others so that you can pass on what you have learned. The group to which the author belonged, met for 19 years. It was nourishment! In fact, it was one of the most important parts of our lives.

FOR GROUPS AND TEACHERS

The Value of a Group is that members may share with each other, learn from each other, discuss questions, and support each other in the practice of Receptive Prayer, in their spiritual growth in general, and in their daily lives. It aids the individual to be faithful to his or her commitment, and pools information which each gathers individually. Sharing things that mean so much, members may well develop friendships for life. Receptive Prayer, experienced in a group, is different in some ways than that which is done alone. There have been many over the ages who have felt an increased power of the presence of God when they worshipped silently and waited for guidance together. As the text points out, the Spirit of God has repeatedly come to individuals receptively yielding to God alone, but the experience of Pentecost demonstrates pointedly how groups of the same mind become a common channel for the Spirit.

Leadership is necessary for the purposes of organization and facilitation to enhance participation and relationships. If someone with experience in meditation from a Christian point of view is available and has gentle leadership qualifications, he or she might be useful in this position.

Commitment of Participants is important. There are three fundamental commitments necessary: the commitment of *being present,* the commitment of *trust,* and the commitment of *daily prayer for each other.* Because a group is formed for the purposes of being together, each member's presence is uniquely necessary to the functioning of the group. Because individuals will be sharing things that are precious, meaningful and perhaps personal, there needs to be a commitment of trust. Because of their desire to support each other spiritually, nothing can be more important than prayer for each other. Until the group experiences this faithful, dependable support, they will not know how strengthening it can be. A spiritual bond will begin to develop which is as real when members are apart as when they are together.

It is important that membership remains stable. New groups may be formed when desired, but relationships already formed are valuable and may be sensitive. If someone leaves and is to be replaced, it is important that everyone feels comfortable about including the new member because of confidences shared.

Logistics include choosing a time and place for the first gathering and personally inviting individuals who would have the deepest interest in such a spiritual journey together. One or two spiritual friends can be a planning nucleus. The most favored size for a group is twelve, but it can be much smaller, though not much larger, and still be effective. The site for meeting should be convenient and the room comfortable, clean, and not too large. Simplicity and beauty in the surroundings are very helpful. A lounge in a church or living room in a home may be just right. It is important that the site be one where there will be no distractions or interruptions. Also, it seems far better to keep a comfortable site for some time after it is chosen. The site itself will grow in meaning to participants.

Invitations or Announcements may be used if preferred. An appropriate text would include the cover statement which is included on page vi: "Most of us pray that..." The invitation to learn Receptive Prayer together, the time and place, and a phone number for questions may be added. The cost for the text and manual should also be included. If you request an RSVP it will enable you to order the text and manual for those who are expected at the first gathering. Having something to read immediately will feed initial enthusiasm.

Useful Resources may be Bibles and hymnals or photo-copies of hymns, copies of the text and manual for everyone, and note-books which individuals will furnish on their own. We have suggested more hymns than necessary because no hymnal contains all of them.

The Introductory Meeting may include:

> Obtaining names, phone numbers, and e-mail addresses, if not yet gathered (These should be copied for everyone to receive at the next meeting);
>
> Providing textbooks and manual;
>
> Getting acquainted by answering one of these questions:
>> "Why am I here?"
>> "What is my passion?"
>> "What is my goal in life?"
>> "What does my devotional life mean to me?"

Introducing Receptive Prayer and saying why it is important;

Allowing questions and discussion;

Consideration and agreement on group aims and commitments, schedule, meeting place, etc.;

Presentation of suggested format for meetings and recommendations for a daily personal format;

A period of worship and receptivity, perhaps based on the 23rd Psalm, and including the singing of the hymn, "The King of Love My Shepherd Is," a reading of the psalm, and participation in the Guided Receptive Prayer entitled: "The Shepherd Psalm" (pp. 133-135 in the text). (Please note: The person leading this worship should acquaint him or herself with suggestions on pp. 132 and 133 of the text, and should have practiced the reading. It needs to be loud enough to be heard by the slightly deaf, yet gentle in tone. Hymnbooks or photo-copied hymns or words should be already available and a pianist or lead singer already chosen and prepared.)

A Suggested Outline of Following Meetings:

A hymn from the lesson studied;

The "Lord of Love" prayer (text, p. 29) followed by several minutes of silence;

Study and discussion of the scripture, then of the text, and, sometimes, the hymn(s);

Sharing of results of Receptive Prayer in the preceding week extemporaneously and/or reading from spiritual journals;

Questions and discussion about the use of Receptive Prayer;

Requests and reports on the use of Receptive Prayer for others;

Guided Receptive Prayer in the form to be followed in the ensuing week;

A blessing of each other through eyes, hands, or words; and

Another hymn, or more if desired. Some extra suggestions are listed in the **HYMNS** section.

Choice of Spiritual Friend or Prayer Partner may be mentioned at the first meeting and the brief paragraph from page 16 in the manual read. Participants may be asked if they would like to form prayer partnerships.

Suggested Introductory Remarks for the First Meeting:

"What we are about to undertake is bound to be one of the most meaningful ventures in our lives. It is a venture that has no end and which leads to horizons that will continue to expand. What we will be studying is very old in the history of religion and of the church, yet new to many. It is natural and spontaneous, yet something we may learn and practice.

"We will be using our brains and our hearts and our sensitivities. We will be making a commitment of time, of trust, and of prayer. We will begin to know each other in ways in which no one else may know us and find support from each other in the fields of devotion and spiritual life where so many travel alone.

"What we will learn, we will continue to be learning for the rest of our lives. The author has put it this way:

'Most of us pray that God will do something *to* us or *for* us,
But God wants to do something *in* us and *through* us.
That can be done only through our cooperation,
Through our *yielding* to God in Receptive Prayer,
First in quietness; then in action. (p. 8)

'When prayer is what it could be, it is:
not monologue, but dialogue; ... (etc., please see page 42 up to "a new, real power to serve and to heal.")

'Meditation in the form of prayer is practical and necessary. The ministry of the church and of individuals will go astray without it. There is no other way to know God's will but to pray and live receptively.' (p.9)

"The most inspiring, powerful, and meaningful experiences in life are related to living and praying in this way. Let us begin."

Regarding Goals and Benefits

Each participant should feel encouraged to accept what he or she receives in Receptive Prayer as personally suitable for him or her in that time and place. It may be a sense of peace or of being loved or the ability to love another more deeply. It may be a new sense of direction or specific guidance, a thought, a plan, or an inspiration. It may be a deep rest or a sense of being in the presence of God. It is important not to feel that the experience of one person should be the identical experience of another. It will not be. Nor will the experience of one day be exactly like another even for the same person.

Sometimes people experience phenomena of inner sight or hearing while they meditate. These are ways that God is using to point out some truth. They can be very valuable, as they were mentioned in the Bible, but they are not important in themselves. If they are sought, rather than simply received, they can become the goal and thus an impediment. Paul spoke of this in I Corinthians 12, 13, and 14.

The goal of Receptive Prayer is to allow God to take over our minds and hearts and lives. It is to be with God, to be in God, and to be God's chalice, channel, and instrument. God is love. Through learning to yield to God, we hope to become God's love for others.

Retreats

To use the material in the Manual for retreats, it would be well to have participants read the textbook ahead of time. The Manual may then be used for the retreat itself.

Since many retreats have less than seven sessions, the leader may choose what is most adaptable to the needs of the groups. However, the author suggests that the first forms of Receptive Prayer suggested in Sections One and Two are those with which it is best to begin.

If a retreat lasts only one or two days, participants may be encouraged to recognize which form speaks to them most effectively at the present time. Then, when they are alone, and not following the group plan, it may be very helpful to concentrate on that one form, allowing its grace to grow in their consciousness, perhaps for several weeks or months.

Hymn Sources

Hymns are listed alphabetically below. After each hymn title is a series of ten numbers or spaces. These refer to twelve hymnals of major denominations which use many of the hymns mentioned. The collections represented are not necessarily the latest hymnal of each denomination, nor is every denomination represented. The span is wide enough, however, to enable everyone who uses the manual to find a copy of most of the hymns mentioned. Blank spaces indicate that that particular hymn is not found in the hymnal to which the blank refers. Additional excellent hymns which are found in only one or two of the suggested hymnals are listed singly at the end of the hymn charts. Sources and hymnals are:

MAN - This Manual.

ELW - *Evangelical Lutheran Worship.* Minneapolis, MN; Augsburg Fortress Publishing House, 2006.

UMH - *The United Methodist Hymnal,* Nashville, TN; The Methodist Publishing House, 1989.

HFG - *Hymns for the Family of God.* Nashville, TN; Paragon Press, 1976.

AAH - *African American Heritage Hymnal.* Chicago, IL; GIA Publications, Inc., 2006.

PH - *The Presbyterian Hymnal.* Louisville, KY; Westminster/ John Knox Press, 1990.

EH - *The Hymnal 1982.* (Episcopal) New York; The Church Hymnal Corp., 1982.

NCH – *The New Century Hymnal.* (The United Church of Christ) Cleveland, OH; Pilgrim Press, 1995.

GA2 - *GATHER: Comprehensive,* Second Edition (Roman Catholic). Chicago, IL; GIA Publications, 2004.

WOV - *With One Voice.* (Lutheran) Minneapolis, MN; Augsburg Fortress, 1995.

LBW - *Lutheran Book of Worship.* Minneapolis, MN and Philadelphia, PA; Augsburg Publishing House and Board of Publication, Lutheran Church in America, 1978.

MH - *The Methodist Hymnal.* Nashville, TN; The Methodist Publishing House, 1964.

SBH - *Service Book and Hymnal.* Minneapolis, MN and Philadelphia, PA; Augsburg Publishing House and Board of Publication, Lutheran Church in America, 1958.

| | | Hymnal | | | | | | | | | |
Hymn	Session	MAN TEXT	ELW	UMH	HFG	AAH	PH	EH	NCH	GA2	WOV
"Alleluia"	1, 5	Text p.96									
"Amazing Grace" (*Native American Languages)	5		448	378*	107	271 272	280*	671	547 548	586	
"Be Thou My Vision"	3		776	451	468		339	488	451		776
"Breathe on Me, Breath of God"	2		SBH 470	420	161	317	316	508	292	800	
"Dear Lord and Father of Mankind"	4		LBW 506	358	422		345	652	502		
"Gather Us In" ("Here In This Place")			718							743	718
"Go My Children, With My Blessing"	7		721						82		721

Hymn	Session	Hymnal									
		MAN TEXT	ELW	UMH	HFG	AAH	PH	EH	NCH	GA2	WOV
"Have Thine Own Way, Lord"	6			382	400	449					
"Here I Am Lord"	4		752	593		567	525			671	752
"How Can I Keep From Singing?"	5		781							598	781
"I Sought the Lord"	5	Man p. 65		341				689			
"I Will Come to You in the Silence"	4		WP 158							627	
"Listen, Listen, God Is Calling"	4		712								712
"Lord, Speak to Me That I May Speak"	4		403	625	344		426		531		
"Mid All the Traffic of the Ways"	4			MH 225	232		322				

103

Hymn	Session	MAN TEXT	ELW	UMH	HFG	AAH	PH	EH	NCH	GA2	WOV
								Hymnal			
"My God, How Wonderful Thou Art"	1, 5		524					643			
"O Jesus, I Have Promised"	4		503	396	493		388 389	655	493	---	
"O Love That Will Not Let Me Go"	7		LBW 324	840	483	290	384	358	485	---	
"On Eagles Wings"	7		779	143						593	779
"Praise the Spirit in Creation"	2							506 507			682
"Spirit of God, Descend Upon My Heart"	1		486	500	147	312	326		290		
"Spirit of the Living God, Fall Afresh on Me"	1	Man p. 23		393	155	320	322		283		

Hymn	Session		MAN TEXT	ELW	UMH	HFG	AAH	PH	EH	NCH	GA2	WOV
							Hymnal					
"Spirit, Spirit of Gentleness"	2			684				319		286		684
"Stay with Us, O Lord"	All		Man p. 24									
"Take My Life, and Let It Be Consecrated"	1			406	399	458		391	707	448		
"Take, O Take Me as I Am"	1		Man p. 24								692	
"Teach Me, My God and King, in All Things Thee to See"	3			SBH 451					592			
"You Satisfy the Hungry Heart" (use for communion)	7			711	629			521			816	711
"You are Mine" "I Have Loved You"				WP 158							504	

BIBLIOGRAPHY ON MEDITATION

(Additions to List in Text)

The Christian Approach

A Monk of the Eastern Church (Lev Gillet). *The Jesus Prayer.* Crestwood, NY: St. Vladimir's Seminary Press, 1987.

Bloom, Archbishop Anthony (Kallistos Ware). *Living Prayer.* Springfield, IL: Templegate Publishers, 1966.

Brame, Grace Adolphsen. "The Prayer Life of Saint Teresa of Avila," Parts I & II, *Sisters Today,* Vol. 58, Nos. 2 & 3, 1986, pp. 98-107, pp. 164-169.

Brame, Grace Adolphsen. "The Prayer of Jesus and Its Relation to Hesychasm and Orthodox Spirituality." *The Patristic and Byzantine Review,* Vol. V, Nos. 1, 2, & 3 (1986) pp. 48-60, 147-154, 222-233.

Clark, Glenn. *The Soul's Sincere Desire.* Boston; Little, Brown, and Co., 1953.

Goettmann, Alphonse and Rachel. *Prayer of Jesus – Prayer of the Heart.* New York and Mahwah, NJ: Paulist Press, 1991.

Hallesby, Ole *Prayer.* Minneapolis, MN: Augsburg Publishing House, 1994.

Hausherr, Irenee. *The Name of Jesus.* Kalamazoo, MI: Cistercian Pubs., 1978.

Keating, Thomas. *Invitation to Love: The Way of Christian Contemplation.* Rockport, MA; Element, 1992.

Keating, Thomas. *Open Heart, Open Mind.* Rockport, MA; Element, 1986.

May, Gerald G. *The Awakened Heart: Opening Yourself to the Love You Need.* San Francisco: HarperSanFrancisco, 1991.

Main, John. *Christian Meditation: Gethsemane Talks,* Tucson, AZ; Medio Media Pub., 1999.

Moffatt, Doris. *Christian Meditation,* Chappaqua, NY; Christian Herald Books, 1979.

Nouwen, Henri J. M. *With Open Hands.* Notre Dame, IN; Ave Maria Press, 2006.

Pennington, M. Basil. *Centering Prayer: Renewing An Ancient Christian Prayer Form.* New York: Image Books, Doubleday, 1980.

Other Approaches

Griffiths, Bede. *Return to the Center.* Springfield, IL; Templegate, *1982.*

The Psychology of Meditation

Froelich, Mary. *The Intersubjectivity of the Mystic:* A Study of Teresa of Avila's *Interior Castle.* Atlanta, GA; Scholars Press, 1993.

Notes to Readers

Comments and suggestions about the use of this material will be welcomed by Charis Enterprises.

Teacher training courses for Receptive Prayer will be held according to demand by Charis Enterprises. With the author teaching, they will be held in Wilmington, DE or at a site chosen by a sponsoring organization. Those interested may write to Charis Enterprises at the address below.

CHARIS ENTERPRISES
13 North Cliffe Drive
Wilmington, DE 19809
Phone (302) 798-2947

WEB SITE for *Dr. Grace Adolphsen Brame* is:

http://www.gracebrame.com
e-mail: grace@gracebrame.com

CPSIA information can be obtained at www.ICGtesting.com
Printed in the USA
LVOW081122140112

263856LV00001B/273/P